# IMPROVE YOUR SURVIVAL SKILLS

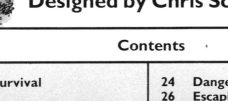

**Lucy Smith**
**Edited by Janet Cook**
**Designed by Chris Scollen**

## Contents

**Survival consultants:**
**John Barry and Mike Holland**

**Illustrated by Paddy Mounter and Chris Lyon**

With thanks to Ken Griffiths

# About survival

In primitive times, every day was a battle for survival. People had to find their own water, food and shelter, so everyone learned the essential skills needed to survive.

Today, we have forgotten many survival skills, since we can buy nearly everything we need.

However, survival situations can still arise: you could be stranded in a snowbound car, lost in unknown country, or a fire could break out in your home. This book shows you some skills which could give you a better chance of surviving such a crisis unharmed.

## Preparing to be a survivor

You can greatly improve your survival chances if you try to keep physically fit. Even half an hour of exercise a day can improve your fitness.

In any survival situation you also need ingenuity, an ability to improvise, and a certain amount of organized thinking to pull you through. You can develop these abilities by imagining yourself in a survival situation and deciding how you would deal with it. Below is some advice on what to do in a crisis.

## Basic survival procedure

If you are caught in a survival situation, try to do the following things immediately:

1. Get yourself and anyone else out of any further danger.

2. Apply first aid (see pages 34-35) if you or anyone else is injured.

3. Move any supplies of equipment, food and water away from danger.

4. Protect yourself physically from the elements by getting into shelter as quickly as possible.

5. Examine the supplies that you have with you and decide what your priorities are: for example, in very hot conditions (see pages 16-17), you may need to look for water right away.

6. Decide whether you are going to stay where you are or try to move to another spot where you are more likely to be rescued (see pages 44-45).

## About this book

In many survival situations you need to find shelter and water. There is advice on how to do this on pages 4-7.

The location and the climate greatly influence what you can and should do in a survival situation. You can find out how to deal with very cold, wet and hot conditions on pages 8-17.

The many possible hazards presented by water are discussed on pages 18-23.

You can find out how to cope with some potentially dangerous creatures on pages 24-25.

While a fire that is out of control is very dangerous, a small camp fire can help you in a crisis. On pages 26-29 you can learn how to escape from a fire, and how to make and control one.

Pages 30-33 discuss how to deal with the dangers that can threaten you in a city or at home.

Pages 34-47 give advice on a wide range of survival skills, such as first aid, self-defense, signaling and finding your way back to safety. You can also find out about survival kits.

Survival situations vary so widely that no book can hope to guarantee that you will survive any situation. However, in reading this book you will almost certainly discover how to help yourself in ways you had not thought of before. In a dangerous situation, who knows, these could be just the extra skills you need to save your life.

## A note about food

If you are inexperienced, it can be very dangerous to eat wild plants. You can easily become poisoned. Trapping animals for food is also risky, since you can get badly bitten. In any case, you can live for up to a month without food, so it should never be your immediate priority in a crisis.

However, food gives you energy and can keep you healthy, so eat well before you go on an expedition, and take some food with you. You can find out what kinds of food to take and how to store them on page 47. Check your supplies regularly to make sure they are still edible.

# Shelter

Shelter is necessary to protect you from the wind, rain, snow and sun*. It also provides the comfort you need in order to sleep, which is vital in giving you physical and mental energy.

If you do not have a tent with you, you will need to build yourself a shelter. There are tips on how to do this below.

## Positioning your camp

The position of your camp can make a lot of difference to its effectiveness. In the picture below, there are a number of tips to remember when choosing a location.

Generally, the lower the camp, the warmer and more sheltered it will be. However, watch out for damp ground at the pit of a valley.

Check that there is no danger from above, for example bees' nests, falling rocks or dead wood.

If possible, camp near water and a supply of wood.

Keep away from solitary trees, as these attract lightning.

Don't camp too close to water – you are likely to be bitten by insects.

Your camp should be easily visible to potential rescue parties.

Camp out of the wind, if possible behind a natural windbreak.

## Setting up camp

The kind of camp you build largely depends on three things:

★ The materials available. These could be natural (such as rocks) or man-made (such as canvas).

★ The weather. For example, if it is likely to rain, you need a roof.

★ How permanent does it need to be? If it is dark, or you are injured, you could build a temporary one.

On the opposite page there are some shelters you could practice making. Then try designing your own.

The ground should be as flat as possible and free of rocks.

## Design requirements

★ Ventilation: so you can breathe properly and avoid getting wet from condensation.

★ Visibility: for finding your way back and attracting potential rescuers.

★ Ease of entrance: so you can get in or out in a hurry.

★ Water and wind resistance.

★ Comfort: you should be able to sit in it.

★ Warmth: the smaller the shelter, the warmer it is.

*You can find out more about shelters for extreme conditions on pages 9, 12 and 16.

## Building a temporary shelter

1. Find or dig a hollow in the ground. Pile up rocks on the side from which the wind is coming. Make a roof with sticks, grass, moss and so on (see above).

2. Turn a plastic sheet into a tent, as shown above. Make a frame with five long sticks, drape the sheet over it and weigh it down with large stones.

## Building a permanent shelter

Follow the steps below to make a secure shelter dome which is comfortable and could last for a few weeks.

Do not exhaust yourself by rushing. You may sweat and then catch a chill as your damp body cools down.

**2. Put the thick end of one stick in the ground on the base outline, then another on the opposite side of the outline. Join them together with string or long, tough grass.**

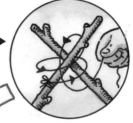

1. Find 16 pliable sticks, about six feet long. Roughly scratch a circle on the ground; it should be approximately six feet in diameter.

**3. Tie another pair of sticks at right angles to the first pair, then tie all four sticks together to make a dome frame.**

5. Weave sticks, grass, moss, leaves, etc. through the frame. For extra protection, cover the whole dome with mud or snow.

**4. Make another dome just below the first, then continue to do this with another two domes. Remember to position them so that there is a gap for the door.**

# Finding and collecting water

The water in your body helps to regulate your temperature, and keep it working properly. It is used up through sweating, urinating and so on, and needs to be replaced. After three days without drinking any water, you would probably die of dehydration. Although carrying water in your survival kit* will reduce any immediate danger, you may need to add to your supply by collecting water from the environment. There are tips on how to do this below.

## How much water do you need?

The chart on the right estimates how much water you need every day, provided you are resting in the shade all day. If you are in full sun or moving around, you need more.

| Temperature | Water needed per day |
|---|---|
| 68°F (20°C) | I liter (2 pints) |
| 77°F (25°C) | 1.2 liters (2.5 pints) |
| 86°F (30°C) | 2.5 liters (5 pints) |
| 95°F (35°C) | 5 liters (10.5 pints) |

## Looking for water

Below are some hints about where you might find water in the environment around you, and how you can use birds and insects to lead you to water.

At low tide, dig shallow holes either side of the high tide mark; there is often a small amount of fresh water just beneath the sand.

Most grain-eating birds (such as finches and pigeons), grazing animals, and flies are signs that water is near.

A group of ants climbing a tree may be heading towards a small pool of trapped water. Make sure they don't bite you.

Dig where there are patches of green vegetation; plants need water to live.

Look in the pit of a valley; rainwater naturally drains down to the bottom of hills.

You could try digging at the outside edge of a dry river bed; a small amount of water is quite likely to collect here.

Look in mountain crevices, where pools of water may be trapped.

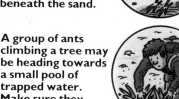

WARNING!!

Don't drink seawater, urine, coffee, tea, or alcohol; they all dehydrate you.

*See pages 46-47 for more about survival kits.

# Collecting water

Rainwater, dew, ice and snow are all good sources of drinking water. Melt ice or snow before drinking, otherwise they will lower your body temperature, and your body will use up water in an attempt to readjust it.

## Rainwater

To catch the maximum amount of rainwater, lean a waterproof container under a tree. Extra water will run down the trunk and into the container.

**Tree**
**Container**

**Plastic**
**Pebbles**

## Dew

To collect dew dig a hole, line the bottom with plastic, then pebbles. Collect the dew early in the morning, before it evaporates, and boil it before drinking (see right).

## Ice or snow

Thinly spread ice or snow on a sheet of plastic (preferably black, as this absorbs the heat). Arrange the plastic to catch the water as it melts.

**Plastic**

**Pan**

## Make a solar still

You can collect at least a pint of water per day using a solar still. Dig a hole, place a container in the center then cover the hole with plastic, seal it around the edge and weight it down with stones. The water in the earth will evaporate, causing droplets to form on the plastic, then fall into the container. The water may attract animals and insects, so check carefully when collecting it.

**Cross-section view**

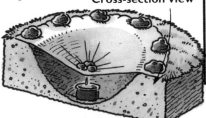

# Purifying the water

There are many serious diseases you could catch from impure water, such as dysentery, cholera, typhoid, worms and leeches. Generally, if you are taking water from a river, the closer you are to the source the better. Treat with suspicion any pool which has nothing growing in it; it is probably polluted.

Although rainwater, snow, ice, and water from a solar still or spring are all pure, any other water should be purified before drinking. Two ways of doing this are shown below.

1. Boil vigorously for at least 15 minutes.

2. Sterilize with iodine or chlorine pills (follow the instructions on the pack carefully)

You can clean water which is particularly dirty by using a filter pump (available in many camping stores) or by straining it through clean canvas, muslin or nylon. Then purify it using one of the methods above.

# Tips on reducing water loss

★ Keep still to reduce sweating.

★ If it is hot, build a shade.

★ Eat little; water is used to digest food.

★ Sleep in shade during the day, and work at night.

★ Breathe through the nose, not the mouth; less moisture will escape.

★ If hot, do not lie on the ground; it can be up to 16.5°C (30°F) hotter on the ground than above it.

★ Wear clothes to protect you from the sun and wind; both cause water to evaporate through the skin.

★ Drink water in sips rather than gulps; guzzling when very thirsty could make you vomit and lose yet more water.

# Keeping warm

Your vital organs, such as your heart and kidneys, need to be kept at a constant temperature of about 37°C (98°F) to function properly. If you are badly equipped, very cold conditions can cause a fall in your body temperature which stops these organs working. This is called hypothermia. Below you can see how to prevent and treat it.

## Clothes

Wearing the right clothes enables you to control the temperature of the air nearest to your body. When dressing for cold conditions remember:

**C:** Clean clothes are warmer than dirty ones: the fibers stand up and trap air better.

**O:** Overheating: avoid this so that you don't sweat. Sweating makes your body and clothes damp and so increases your chances of becoming chilled (see below). If you get too hot, shed some clothes.

**L:** Layers of clothes are the best protection against cold. They trap air next to your body and between clothes: this air is kept still and warm, acting as an insulator. The more layers you wear, the warmer you will be.

**D:** Dry: keep that way. You lose body heat much faster if you are damp or wet. To stop damp getting in from outside in cold, wet conditions, your outer layer of clothing should be completely waterproof.*

Hat

Insulating jacket (3)

Waterproof jacket (4)

Scarf

Wool socks (1)

Leg-warmers

Thick pants (2)

Boots

Wool shirt (2)

Goggles

Lip balm

Mitts

Medium weight sweaters (3)

Wool vest (1)

### Layers to wear

1 Underwear. This should carry body moisture away from your skin into layer **2** (see below).

2 Clothing. This absorbs moisture from **1**, which is then evaporated by warm air trapped between **2** and **3**.

3 Insulation. This keeps your body even warmer by trapping more air.

4 Shell. This is the crucial outer layer which protects you from the elements. It should be both windproof and waterproof.

*On page 11 there are more tips on how to avoid getting wet in cold conditions.

# Shelters for cold conditions

A shelter is crucial if you are stranded in cold conditions. It should be small and protect you on all sides, to keep the air still and warm.*

## Natural shelters

◀ Look for places such as caves, or the sheltered area under evergreen trees (see left). Watch out, though, for trees that are heavily laden with snow. In cold weather their frozen branches may snap under the weight.

**Air gap**  **Treepit shelter**

### Making a snow hole shelter

If you are in a place where thick snow has ▶ piled up in packed drifts** you can build a snow hole. You will need a shovel to dig with.

1. Dig a short tunnel into the snowdrift, heading slightly down, then up again. Don't dig so hard you tire yourself out.

2. At the end of the tunnel, scoop out a chamber in the snow. Shave the roof smooth and glaze it with a lit candle so it doesn't drip. Make a ventilation hole in the roof. Mark the outside of the shelter.

3. Build a ledge out of snow, above the level of the tunnel, to put your bed on. Make sure you leave about 4ft between the ledge and the roof, so that you have enough room to sit upright.

**Air hole**  **Chamber (about 8ft)**  **Candle**

**Dip traps cold air.**  **Ledge raises bed above dip where it is warmer.**

**Tunnel (about 3ft)**

## Shelter tips

1. Make sure that the exit and air holes of the shelter are kept clear of snow so you can breathe.

2. Burn a candle (see page 46) in the shelter to give warmth and light.

3. Keep tools in the shelter to dig yourself out if you get snowed in.

4. Stay inside the shelter unless you absolutely have to go out: it is warmer inside.

# Hypothermia

Hypothermia is usually caused by a combination of factors including cold, wind, wet, and exhaustion. These all contribute to a drop in your body temperature. Hypothermia symptoms include:

**Feeling cold**  **Unconsciousness**
⬇  ⬆
**Shivering**
⬇  **Collapse**
**Slower reflexes**  ⬆
⬇  **Blurred vision**
**Loss of balance**

## Hypothermia dos and don'ts

| Never: | Instead: |
|---|---|
| ★ Never rub your body to try to warm yourself up. | ★ Get into shelter immediately. |
| ★ Never drink alcohol. | ★ Get into a sleeping bag, insulated from the ground by dry bedding. |
| ★ Never warm yourself up very close to a fire. | ★ Wrap yourself in as many layers as possible. |
| These activities reopen the surface blood vessels, sending icy blood straight back to the vital organs. | ★ If possible, huddle close to a friend for body warmth. |
| ★ Never keep walking: you use up vital energy. | ★ Take warm drinks such as broth or sugared tea. |

*On pages 4-5 you can find more advice about making shelters.
**Watch out for areas where avalanches are likely (see page 10).

# Environmental hazards

In very snowy conditions, avalanches are a major potential hazard in hilly or mountainous places. Below you can find out more about them, how they start, and possible danger areas. There are also tips on what to do if you get caught in one. On the opposite page there is advice on avoiding the chilling effects of wind and dampness, and on what to do if you are stranded in a snowbound car.

**Avalanches have been known to travel at around 250 mph.**

## Avalanches

Avalanches occur when heavy snow which has gathered in high places suddenly cascades downwards with great force. They can kill by suffocating or injuring you. They occur in areas with snow-covered slopes, especially mountainous regions. Slopes that bulge outward, where the snow can slip, or ones that are sheltered, where the snow may not freeze and pack solid, are particularly dangerous. Keep out of deep valleys surrounded by steep snowy sides: in an avalanche, all the snow would pelt down into the valley.

### How an avalanche can start

★ Loud noises. These cause vibrations that can loosen snow.

★ Heavy snowfalls. Allow at least a day for fresh snow to settle before you venture out near steep slopes.

★ Falling rocks at the top of snowy slopes.

★ Sun on snow can thaw and loosen it.

★ A rainfall or sudden rise in temperature may thaw and loosen snow.

### If you are caught in an avalanche:

★ Get rid of all your equipment: this could injure you or hamper your movements.

★ Try to get to the side of the avalanche.

★ Lie as flat as possible and try to "swim" backstroke on top of the avalanche, facing uphill to protect your head.

★ Keep your mouth shut and, if possible, cover your nose: you can drown by inhaling snow.

★ As the avalanche stops, cup your hands over your face to make an air space.

★ When it stops, clear as big a space as possible around you before the snow freezes and sets. Quickly try to get up to the surface.

★ Conserve your energy and try not to panic, since this makes your body use up extra oxygen.

## Snowbound in a car

A car trip in snowy conditions could result in you becoming snowbound. Always take a car survival kit (see pages 46-47) on such journeys. If the car gets snowbound:

1. Stay with the car. It gives you some shelter and is much easier for rescuers to spot.

2. Get all useful things, such as blankets, out of the trunk immediately.

3. Tie a bright cloth to the antenna as a marker or fasten something visible to the roof.

4. Avoid getting tired, damp and cold by trying to dig the car out or push it.

5. Run the engine as little as possible and then only if the exhaust is clear of snow. Otherwise, there is a risk of carbon monoxide poisoning from the exhaust fumes.

6. Always keep a fresh air supply available. Open a window slightly, on the side away from the wind. In deep snowdrifts, poke an air passage up to the surface with a pole or shovel handle.

## The effect of the wind

Wind makes the temperature seem much cooler than it actually is, because it blows all the body heat away from any parts of you that are exposed. The chart below shows you the difference this effect, called the windchill factor, makes to how cold you feel. As you can see, the windchill factor depends on how cold it is, and on the speed of the wind.

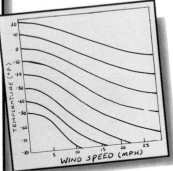

### Avoiding the wind

Keep on the sheltered side of ridges, out of the wind. Stay off open heights, such as hilltops, where you are more exposed. Never travel during a blizzard: it can chill and exhaust you.

## The effect of the wet

Try to avoid getting wet if it is cold, especially if it is also windy. You lose body heat very fast when damp and it is difficult to get dry again in cold conditions.

### Avoiding the wet

★ If caught in heavy rain or snow, stop and shelter until conditions improve.

★ Keep out of deep snow. It can make you very wet and is exhausting to travel through.

★ Snow is usually softer, wetter and deeper in stretches of woodland. It is more sheltered there and so may not harden.

★ Don't cross rivers or streams. Entering cold water can kill (see page 18). Keep off ice.

★ When the temperature rises, snow melts. Beware of ground which has become marshy or water logged. You may sink into the mud, making traveling difficult (see page 15).

# Shelter and clothing

Although rain can be refreshing, it can also be dangerous if you are unprepared. If it is wet and cold, you may develop hypothermia (see pages 8-9). The warm, wet conditions of the tropics present other dangers (see page 14). Below there is advice about protecting yourself in very wet conditions.

## Shelters for wet conditions

If you see signs of rain coming, get into shelter immediately. If there is no convenient shelter available, build one following the tips on pages 4-5 and these suggestions.

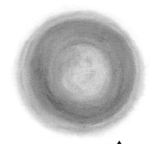

**Hang layers so that sides slope at steep angles and water runs away.**

**Two layers: second layer fits inside first.**

★ Ideally, the roof and sides should be made of a waterproof material. However, non-waterproof fabrics can keep out water if they are closely woven and properly arranged (see above).

★ Make sure you rig the roof high enough to accommodate a raised bed. This is vital to protect you from the ground, which can become waterlogged and in tropical areas may be crawling with insects.

In mild conditions, pile up dry materials (see page 5) and place plastic sheeting between these and your bedding. In tropical conditions you will need to make a proper raised platform for your bed (see below), which should be between 1ft-3ft off the ground.

**Upright log frame supports "mattress".**

**"Mattress" made of branches.**

**Layers of palm leaves**

**Whole structure covered with tarpaulin.**

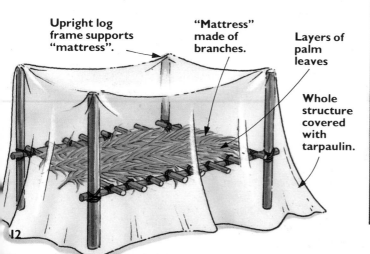

## Signs of rain

There are several ways of telling that a downpour is likely. Look out for the following signs:

★ A red sky in the morning.

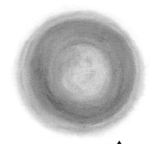

★ A misty glow or ring round the sun or moon.

★ A sky that is overcast with greyish cloud in the evening. This means rain will soon fall.

★ Mist or cloud that does not clear from mountains or hilly places by the middle of the day often becomes rain by the end of the afternoon.

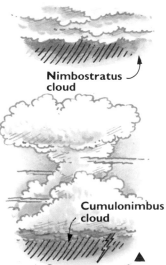

**Nimbostratus cloud**

**Cumulonimbus cloud**

★ Certain types of clouds, such as cumulonimbus. These are dark and low-hanging, often with paler cloud building up immediately above them. They indicate stormy weather.

Nimbostratus clouds mean that rain will fall within the next few hours. They form dark, flat sheets of cloud, creating an overcast, gloomy sky.

## Clothing for wet conditions

Make sure that your "shell" layer* is fully waterproof. Heavily coated nylon is a cheap and effective

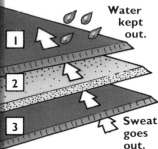

Water kept out.

Sweat goes out.

waterproof fabric. You can also buy clothes made of more expensive fabrics which not only stop water from getting in, but also allow sweat from inside to pass out: this stops you from getting soaked by any sweat that has condensed inside your outer layer.

### Clothing tips

★ Always carry spare dry clothes stored in a waterproof bag.

★ Avoid cotton clothes, which absorb and retain a lot of moisture.

★ Make sure you cover every part of your body.

★ Don't wear tight trousers if it is wet: they will stick to you and can freeze in the cold.

★ To stop wet clothes from freezing overnight, wrap them in plastic and put them in your sleeping bag.

### What to do if you get soaked

Don't travel too far in wet clothes if it is also windy and cold, or you may suffer from hypothermia. Instead, stop and take shelter. Then change into your spare dry clothes. If you feel cold, get into your sleeping bag. Make sure you don't get the bag wet, or it won't insulate properly. When the weather clears up, dry your wet clothes in the sun, or tie them to your outside layer so they dry in the breeze as you walk.

### Bivouac bags

A bivouac bag made from a waterproof fabric gives you some immediate protection from the cold, wind, and wet. To use it, you simply get inside and zip it up.

*See page 8 for details about the "shell" layer.

# Tropical regions and swamps

Tropical regions and swampy areas are particularly wet and waterlogged, and present specific hazards, some of which are discussed below. A small fire can help protect you from some of these dangers, for example by driving insects away, or drying damp clothes. Opposite there are tips about making a fire in wet conditions.*

## The tropics

In tropical jungles (such as those in parts of South America, Africa, and Asia), temperatures are high (often 37°C, or 98F), there is frequent and very heavy rain, and the air is very humid. Dense vegetation makes traveling difficult and the jungle is often teeming with insects which may bite and can transmit disease.

If you are venturing into the tropical jungle, follow the tips below.

**Krait (a very poisonous snake).**

## Tropical dos and don'ts

★ Do shake out your clothes, boots, sleeping bags and equipment before putting them on or using them, to make sure no insects or snakes** got into them.

★ Do treat any injuries immediately. Germs breed fast in warm, damp conditions and even small cuts can easily become infected.

★ Do keep your body covered. Make sure your clothes are fastened at the collar and cuffs to stop mosquitoes and other insects from getting in.

★ Don't leave your clothes or boots lying around on the ground where dangerous creatures may crawl into them.

★ Don't leave food or drinking water lying around uncovered. They may become infested with insects which can spread disease.

★ Don't exert yourself too much. The heat and humidity sap your energy and continuous walking will make you sweat, attracting insects hungry for salt.

*Make sure you read pages 28-29 on fire-making as well.
**You can find out more about dangerous animals on pages 24-25.

## Swamps and marshes

You can usually tell if the ground is marshy by looking at the vegetation. There may be tufts of bright green grass or reeds growing quite far apart. Try to avoid venturing into marshland: traveling across the bogs is difficult and exhausting. As well as getting soaked and muddy, you are likely to be plagued by mosquitoes and other insects which gather in marshy areas.

### If you start to sink into a swamp or marsh:

#### Don't

★ Don't panic: you CAN get free.

★ Don't aim to stay on your feet: trying to pull one leg free from the mud will make you push the other further in.

★ Don't struggle wildly: you will only push yourself further under and become exhausted.

#### Instead

1. Get rid of any equipment that may hamper your movements and weigh you down. If possible, spread a jacket or blanket over a wide area just in front of you.

2. Spread your body over as wide a surface area as possible by sinking to your knees and then dropping gently on to your front. Make sure you keep your head above the surface.

3. "Swim", preferably using a slow breaststroke action, and try to lever with your body gently as you go so that you can kick your feet free. Then try to roll out on to firm ground.

**Mosquitoes**

## Making a fire in wet conditions

Look for ground which has been shielded from the rain to use as the site. Don't light your fire right at the foot of a tree, which could catch fire. If there is no dry ground, build a platform on which to base the fire. You can use a layer of dry logs, covered with some earth, as a basic platform.

If the ground is waterlogged, you will need a higher platform. This sort of fire is called a temple fire (see below).

**Four sticks stuck in ground to make a square.**

**Thinner sticks tied to these as cross supports.**

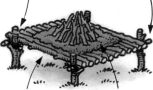

**Layer of logs rests on cross supports.**

**Layer of earth covers logs.**

Clear away any wet rocks or stones from the fireplace. The heat can make these expand and shatter, and the flying pieces could hurt you.

You need dry fuel: choose wood that has not been lying on the ground or that has been in a sheltered spot. You must also have some waterproof matches and a piece of dry striking paper (see page 46) to light the fire.

# Survival in hot conditions

Just as it can be fatal if your body temperature falls below a certain level (see pages 8-9), you may suffer from heatstroke if you are exposed to extreme heat for a long period without water. You get heatstroke when your body becomes overheated and its natural cooling system fails. You stop sweating, your skin becomes hot and dry, and you may become unconscious and die if left untreated. Below you can find out how to survive very hot conditions.

## Water

You must have water to survive for any length of time in hot conditions. In normal conditions you need about four and a half pints a day, but this can rise to as much as 14 pints a day in very high temperatures. Even if you keep still and don't eat, your digestive and cooling systems can cause water losses of up to nine pints a day.

There is lots of advice on finding and conserving water on pages 6-7. If you are in a desert or a hot, arid region, follow these extra suggestions:

★ Don't ration your water intake; if you have water and are thirsty, drink it. Your body cannot adapt to having less water than it needs and it is better to store water inside your body than outside it.

★ Travel by night or early in the morning, before the sun is at its height. It will be much cooler.

★ Stay in the shade and keep still or sleep during the heat of the day: you will use up less energy and water.

## Shelter

If you are stranded in hot conditions, get into shelter from the sun immediately. Don't use up a lot of energy and water by trying to construct a permanent shelter during the heat of the day. Use natural shelter such as the shade at the base of rocky outcrops, or make a very simple shelter such as those shown here.

**Roof with two layers**

**Air space between layers means less heat reaches you.**

**Shallow trench**

In deserts, it is cooler a few inches below the surface of the sand. For a quick shelter, dig a shallow trench in the sand. Lie in it and cover yourself with a sheet or space blanket (see pages 46-47), with the reflective side facing towards the sun.

Temperatures in the desert can drop rapidly at night. The shelter on the right will protect you from both heat and cold.

Use a large sheet of material such as canvas, draped over some kind of support. During the day, raise the bottom of the sheet slightly and fold it back so that air can circulate better. At night, use stones to hold the edges down.

**Fold flaps back to keep cool.**

## Clothes

Keep as much of your body as possible covered in layers of thin, loose-fitting clothes. These protect you from the sun and allow air to circulate. Wear light-colored clothes. These reflect the sun's rays instead of absorbing them. At night, you may need extra clothes in the desert as temperatures fall.

Make sure you shade your eyes, face and neck by wearing a wide-brimmed, light-colored hat or by making a burnoose (see below). A burnoose protects your face and neck and keeps out sand and grit blown by sandstorms.

### Making a burnoose

1. Put wad of cloth on head.

2. Place second piece of cloth over wad.

3. Fasten with strip of cloth or headband.

4. Wrap more cloth round lower face.

Protect your eyes from the glare. If you have no sunglasses, improvise protection by cutting slits in a piece of cloth, bark or cardboard and tying this round your head to make goggles.

Keep your feet and lower legs well covered when traveling on foot. Hot sand can badly burn and blister the soles of your feet and the sun may burn the tops. Wear socks under boots or wind cloth round your feet and ankles to stop sand and insects from getting in.

**Goggles**

**Covered feet.**

## Desert dangers

Two particular threats to watch out for in deserts are flash floods and dust devils.

**Wadi or dried-up riverbed**

### Flash floods

Flash floods occur when a burst of very heavy rain strikes straight to the desert floor, since there is little vegetation to disperse it. The ground is usually baked so hard that it cannot absorb the water, which therefore pours along any available channels, gathering great speed and depth and transforming a dry riverbed into a seething torrent in just one minute. Never shelter in wadis (dried-up riverbeds) or gullies. If you are traveling along one when it starts to rain, climb out on to the bank immediately.

### Dust devils

Whirlwinds known as dust ▶ devils occur quite frequently in the desert. They sweep sand and grit around at great speed.

If you see black clouds gathering or the air becomes very dusty, take shelter immediately and cover yourself up. Be particularly careful to cover your face and eyes.

# The main dangers and saving yourself

Water is a completely different environment from land and so presents human beings with some of the hardest survival challenges.

Below you can learn about the main dangers of water and how to cope if you find yourself in the water without equipment to help you.

## The main dangers

### Drowning
If you inhale even a small amount of water, you may drown, because any water that enters your lungs can damage them so that they cannot function effectively. Water in your windpipe can also make it go into a spasm, preventing you from breathing.
Hypothermia, shock and exhaustion can all lead to drowning as they may stop you from keeping your head above water.

### Shock
The shock of suddenly entering cold water can kill you. Try to go in gradually so your body has time to adjust to the different temperature.

### Exhaustion
Vigorous swimming or splashing around saps your energy and eventually exhausts you. In a crisis, move as little as you can: just enough to keep yourself afloat.

### Hypothermia
Hypothermia (see pages 8-9) is a risk as you lose body heat more quickly in water than on land. Keep as still as you can while staying afloat: moving water takes heat away faster than still water.

## Survival tips

1. You must know how to swim properly. If you can't swim already, learn now. Make sure you are taught by an experienced swimmer and only practice in a safe environment with someone to supervise you.

2. Use a survival swimming method (see opposite) to stay afloat while moving as little as possible.

3. If you are with anyone else, huddle together: the heat produced by your bodies will keep you warmer.

4. You lose about 20% of your body heat through your head, and this is aggravated if your face keeps getting wet. Tread water (see opposite) and turn away from the waves to keep your face drier.

5. For warmth, it is best to keep all your clothes on except any you need to use as a buoyancy aid (see opposite).

# Survival swimming*

In many water survival situations it is more important for you to stay afloat for a long time rather than to cover much distance. These survival swimming techniques show you how to keep afloat using as little energy as possible.

## Drownproofing

**Keep mouth closed.**

**Press arms down slightly.**

1. Take a deep breath and hold it. Relax your body into a half-tucked position, with your face underwater.

2. As you begin to run out of breath, breathe out quickly through your nose into the water. Keep mouth closed.

**Keep legs still.**

**Close mouth again.**

3. Gently raise your head clear of the water. Breathe in deeply through your mouth only.

4. Holding this breath, close your mouth. Lower face back into water. Repeat sequence as before.

## Treading water

1. Start with your body relaxed but upright. Hold your head clear of the water. Keep your legs directly under your body. Hold your arms on a level with your chest.

2. To support yourself in this position, pedal your legs slowly in circles in the water, as if you were riding a bicycle. Don't move quickly: this makes your body lose heat faster.

3. It may also help if you move your arms slowly, pressing the water gently down and away from you. Try to relax and move with a smooth, calm and rhythmic action.

# Improvising a buoyancy aid

Improvising a buoyancy aid out of a piece of clothing can also help you to stay afloat. You may have to tread water to start with, to keep your head up as you inflate the aid. Below you can see how to use a pair of pants as a buoyancy aid.

1. Take the trousers off. Tie the legs together tightly at the cuffs, using your teeth to help you as you pull the knot tight. Then hold the pants behind your head by the waistband.

2. Inflate the pants by holding the waistband open and swinging them smoothly up in an arc over your head and straight down into the water. They should fill with air.

3. Now hold the waistband pressed tightly shut against your chest, to keep the air in the pants. Put your head between the legs, with the knotted cuffs behind your neck.

*There is no ideal survival swimming method. Drownproofing saves energy but increases heat loss through the face. Treading water keeps the face dry, but uses up more energy.*

# Be prepared

You can often reduce the dangers of water if you are properly prepared. Always try to find out about any environmental hazards (see pages 22-23) if you are going into an unknown area. Tell people where you are going and when you hope to return.

Below there are lots of tips on how best to prepare yourself.

## Equipment and clothing

Ask an expert about the specific equipment and clothing you need if you are learning a water sport. In this picture you can see some examples of essential equipment to take if you go out in a boat (B) or for a swim (S).

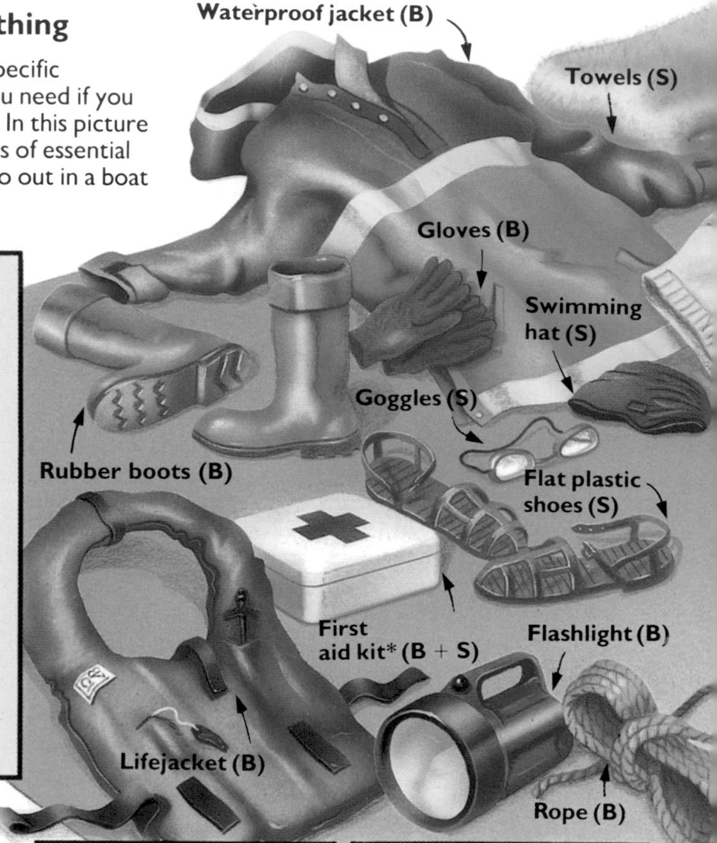

Waterproof jacket (B)

Towels (S)

Gloves (B)

Swimming hat (S)

Goggles (S)

Flat plastic shoes (S)

Rubber boots (B)

First aid kit* (B + S)

Flashlight (B)

Lifejacket (B)

Rope (B)

## Equipment tips

Always try to remember these three general rules:

1. Have the right equipment.

2. Know how and when to use it and where you have stored it.

3. Look after it: check it before each trip to make sure it works properly.

Brightly colored equipment is easier for rescuers to spot in the water.

## Lifejackets

Lifejackets are the safest kind of flotation device** because they inflate so that your head is kept above water even if you are knocked unconscious. Make sure you know how to put on and inflate your lifejacket quickly and properly: speed is often crucial in survival situations.

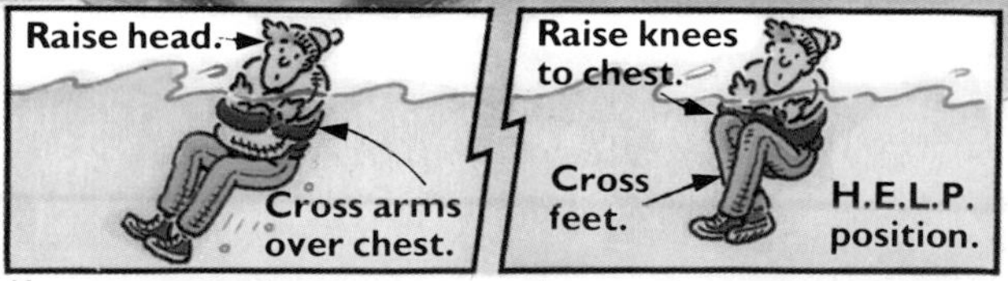

Raise head. Cross arms over chest.

Raise knees to chest. Cross feet. H.E.L.P. position.

If you are wearing a lifejacket and have to keep yourself afloat in cold water for a long time, use the Heat Escape Lessening Position (H.E.L.P.) shown above to prevent hypothermia (see page 8). This keeps your head, chest and groin, which all lose most heat, covered up.

*You can find out what to put in a first aid kit on page 35.
**Flotation devices are things designed to help you float, such as buoyancy aids and lifejackets.

## Wetsuits

A wetsuit is a close-fitting waterproof suit which works by trapping a layer of water between the suit and your skin. This layer warms up gradually and acts as an insulator. Wetsuits are useful if you are going to spend a long time in water.

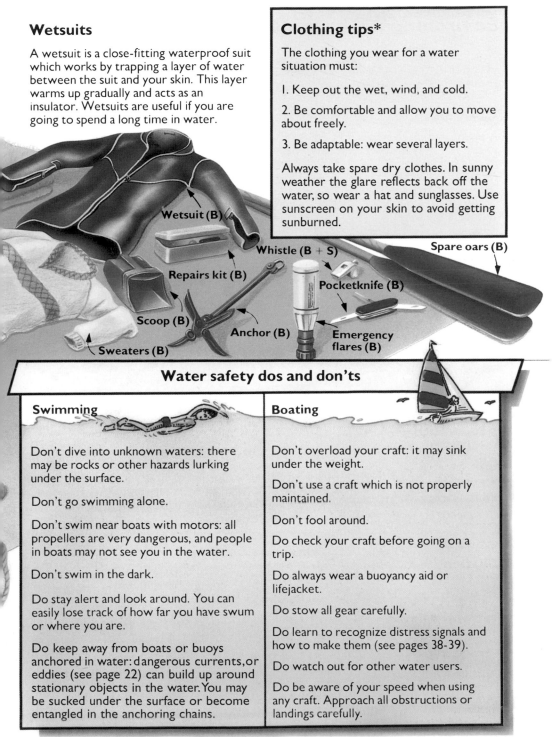

Wetsuit (B)

Repairs kit (B)

Scoop (B)

Sweaters (B)

Anchor (B)

Whistle (B + S)

Pocketknife (B)

Emergency flares (B)

Spare oars (B)

## Clothing tips*

The clothing you wear for a water situation must:

1. Keep out the wet, wind, and cold.

2. Be comfortable and allow you to move about freely.

3. Be adaptable: wear several layers.

Always take spare dry clothes. In sunny weather the glare reflects back off the water, so wear a hat and sunglasses. Use sunscreen on your skin to avoid getting sunburned.

## Water safety dos and don'ts

### Swimming

Don't dive into unknown waters: there may be rocks or other hazards lurking under the surface.

Don't go swimming alone.

Don't swim near boats with motors: all propellers are very dangerous, and people in boats may not see you in the water.

Don't swim in the dark.

Do stay alert and look around. You can easily lose track of how far you have swum or where you are.

Do keep away from boats or buoys anchored in water: dangerous currents, or eddies (see page 22) can build up around stationary objects in the water. You may be sucked under the surface or become entangled in the anchoring chains.

### Boating

Don't overload your craft: it may sink under the weight.

Don't use a craft which is not properly maintained.

Don't fool around.

Do check your craft before going on a trip.

Do always wear a buoyancy aid or lifejacket.

Do stow all gear carefully.

Do learn to recognize distress signals and how to make them (see pages 38-39).

Do watch out for other water users.

Do be aware of your speed when using any craft. Approach all obstructions or landings carefully.

*See pages 8 and 13 for details of the best types of fibes and layers to wear.

# Environmental hazards

Water movement changes according to currents and weather conditions. Below there is advice on how to spot signs of danger in and near the water and how to deal with certain critical situations.

## Currents

A strong current can easily sweep you away, so learn to spot places where currents may be particularly strong or slack. The diagram below shows you some general principles.

## Tides

Tides make seawater rise or fall as well as pulling it away from or towards the shore. It takes about six hours for a high tide (when the water is inshore) to change to a low tide (when the water is out). The tide pulls at its strongest during the third and fourth hours, so try to avoid being caught out at this time. Check the times of the tide changes with people who know the area.

## Winds

If you are going out on water, check the strength and direction of the wind. To check the direction, look at stationary boats out on the water, and also at exposed trees and flags on dry land, to see which way they are being blown. Wind is usually stronger on open water and round exposed headlands. Dark patches of ripples moving across the surface, and wave crests being blown off in a cloud of spray, also indicate strong gusts.

**Slower current in shallow water.**

**Faster current in deeper water.**

**Slower current on inside of bend.**

**Faster current on outside of bend.**

**Fast current through narrower gaps.**

**Back eddy* filling in gaps.**

**Back eddy below island.**

**Fast current round headlands.**

## Dos and don'ts

Do learn as much as you can about the currents and tides in the area before going in or on the water.

Do check the weather forecast for the rest of the day to find out if storms or strong winds are likely.

Do look out for potential danger areas. Make sure you know what the hazards are (see opposite).

Don't set out in a strong offshore wind. It can blow you into dangerous areas and you may not be able to get back to shore.

Don't set out in an onshore wind if there are rocks by the shore. The wind could drive you back on to them.

Don't swim against a current if you can avoid it. It is easier to swim diagonally across it until you reach slacker water.

*A fixed obstruction in a current causes some water to flow back against the main current. This water flow is called an eddy and can be quite strong.

## Potential danger areas

### Docks

These are often crowded with boats, so stay out of the water. Keep away from the dockside, which may be unprotected. Beware of tripping over ropes and falling in.

### Reservoirs and lakes

Reservoirs and lakes often have outflow points where the water runs into a fast-flowing river or over a weir. Keep away from these, as you can be swept away if you fall in.

### Seaside

Don't swim out in heavy surf. The returning water flows out to sea under the incoming waves, creating a dangerous undertow which can pull you under.

### Ice

Never play on frozen water. You can easily fall through and suffer shock, or be trapped under the ice.

### Dams and weirs

These usually produce dangerous currents. They may also have steep, smooth sides which are easy to slip down and very difficult to climb out on to.

### Rivers

Watch out on the banks, which may be slippery and very steep. Don't wade across: the water is usually very cold and you may suffer shock (see page 18). You could also be sucked downstream by strong currents.

## Water survival situations

### Escaping from weirs

If swept towards a weir from upstream, dive down to the riverbed, where the current is weaker, and swim for the bank. If trapped in the turbulence just below a weir, dive down. The current will throw you clear from underneath.

### Adrift at sea

1. Never leave the craft. It keeps you out of the water and offers you some shelter.

2. Keep bailing out any water that gets in.

3. Signal for help (see pages 38-39). Make the craft easy to spot (see below).

4. Ration all food from the start.

### Capsizal

1. Hold on to the craft. The boat supports you and is much easier for rescuers to see than a lone person in the water.

2. Inflate your lifejacket fully as soon as you can.

3. Fasten some bright clothing to the craft to make it easy for potential rescuers to spot.

# Dangerous creatures

Although many animals are potentially dangerous, most are wary of human beings and will withdraw if given the chance. Keep your distance and you are unlikely to be attacked. Below there is advice on how to avoid provoking an animal attack and what to do if you encounter such creatures as sharks or snakes.

## Dos and don'ts

Do be particularly careful at night. Most animals are more active then.

Do keep calm. Animals can sense when you are frightened, and may become more aggressive.

Do treat all wild animals with respect. Most are quicker, more agile and may be stronger than you.

Do watch where you tread, particularly in overgrown areas or in the sea. Many injuries arise from people stepping on animals by accident.

Don't try to play with, feed, touch, tame, catch or tease wild animals.

Don't try to take young animals from their nests: a normally placid animal may kill to protect its young.

Don't leave food and drink lying around. Animals are drawn to these and a hungry creature may be more savage.

Don't make sudden movements or loud noises near wild animals unless they can get away from you. A cornered, frightened animal will be more aggressive.

## Snakes

Snakes usually only bite if stepped on, cornered, seized or guarding their young. However, all snakebites are potentially dangerous. Even if the snake is not venomous, the bite can become infected. On the right are some poisonous snakes.

**Bushmaster**

**Coral snakes**

### Precautions:

★ Shake out equipment before using and don't leave it on the ground.

★ Before putting your hand into bushes or holes, or picking up logs, prod them with a stick to drive out hidden snakes.

★ Stay alert, especially when walking over rocky slopes or through thick undergrowth. Snakes are often well camouflaged and can strike quickly if surprised.

★ Cover your feet and legs: even thin pants can give vital protection against a snake fangs.

★ Learn about the types and habits of the snakes native to the areas you are visiting, so you know which particular ones to watch out for.

### If you are bitten:

Wash away venom that is on the skin. If you have a bandage, wind it tightly above and around the bite, trying to keep the affected part still and lower than your heart. This slows down the poisoned blood returning to the heart and so limits the spread of the poison through the blood system. Get medical help.

## Sharks

**Great white shark**

Despite their bad reputation, sharks rarely attack people. Most sharks live and feed in very deep water, so you are unlikely to encounter one while you are swimming. However, if you see a shark in shallow water, beware: it has probably followed its prey there and is more likely to attack, since it may be hungry.

If you are in water where sharks are known to be active, follow the precautions below.

### Precautions

★ In a boat, don't clean fish at the side or trail your hands and feet in the water.

★ Don't keep swimming if you are injured: sharks are drawn to the smell of blood.

★ Don't swim alone: sharks are less likely to attack a group of people.

★ Don't swim at night, dawn and dusk, when sharks are most active.

★ Always observe any shark warnings.

### Shark attack

A shark may be about to attack if it begins to circle inwards towards you suddenly. In which case:

★ Try to leave the water using strong, regular movements. Weak, splashing movements may suggest wounded, easy prey.

★ If the shark continues to follow you, keep swimming away and try to change direction sharply as you go: sharks often cannot veer fast enough to keep up.

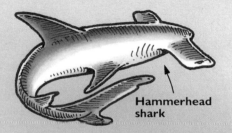

**Hammerhead shark**

★ If you cannot get away, slap the surface of the water and shout: loud noises may deter the shark. Jab it on the top of its snout with a paddle, your foot or fist.

## Mosquitoes

Mosquitoes are common in areas with stagnant water or in hot, damp conditions. They are particularly active at night. Though tiny, in some areas they carry malaria or other dangerous fevers which you may contract if they bite you.

You can keep mosquitoes at bay by lighting a fire (smoke may repel them) and wearing adequate clothes.*

★ **Wear a mosquito net over your head and neck.**

★ **A mosquito can bite through thin clothes, so wear several layers.**

★ **Make sure all clothes are well fastened at wrists, ankles and neck.**

*See also pages 14-15 and 17.

# Escaping from fire

Fire can spread at terrifying speed. If one breaks out, your main priority should be to get to safety and alert other people. However, in certain circumstances, for example if you are on the spot when a fire starts, you may be able to extinguish it before it threatens your safety.

Below you will find advice on what to do to help ensure that you survive a fire.

## Escaping a fire in the home

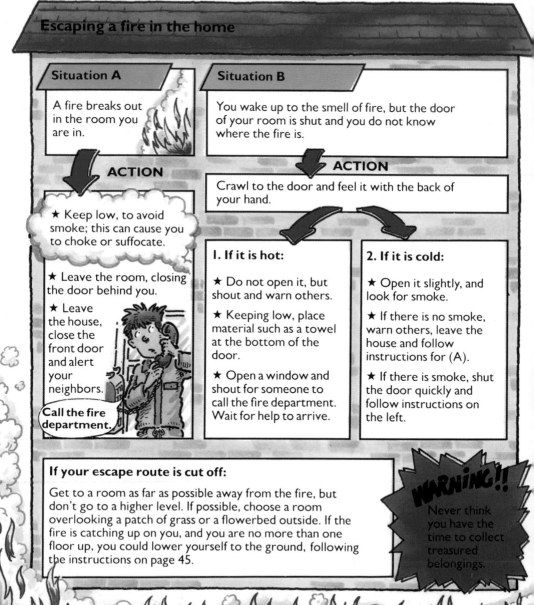

### Situation A

A fire breaks out in the room you are in.

**ACTION**

★ Keep low, to avoid smoke; this can cause you to choke or suffocate.

★ Leave the room, closing the door behind you.

★ Leave the house, close the front door and alert your neighbors.

**Call the fire department.**

### Situation B

You wake up to the smell of fire, but the door of your room is shut and you do not know where the fire is.

**ACTION**

Crawl to the door and feel it with the back of your hand.

**1. If it is hot:**

★ Do not open it, but shout and warn others.

★ Keeping low, place material such as a towel at the bottom of the door.

★ Open a window and shout for someone to call the fire department. Wait for help to arrive.

**2. If it is cold:**

★ Open it slightly, and look for smoke.

★ If there is no smoke, warn others, leave the house and follow instructions for (A).

★ If there is smoke, shut the door quickly and follow instructions on the left.

### If your escape route is cut off:

Get to a room as far as possible away from the fire, but don't go to a higher level. If possible, choose a room overlooking a patch of grass or a flowerbed outside. If the fire is catching up on you, and you are no more than one floor up, you could lower yourself to the ground, following the instructions on page 45.

**WARNING!!**
Never think you have the time to collect treasured belongings.

# Forest fires

Check which way the wind is blowing (look at the direction of the smoke), and plan your escape route as follows:

1. If the wind is blowing away from you, towards the fire, the fire will be slowed down slightly. Head into the wind and try to find a natural gap in the trees, ideally a river.

2. If the wind is blowing towards you, you will have to move very quickly as the fire will be traveling fast (speeds of over 5mph have been recorded). If possible, try to go around the fire, but if it is very wide and it catches up with you, try to take refuge in a deep gulley or ditch.

**Do not move upwards; fire travels faster when going uphill.**

**Many forests are divided by broad paths, designed to stop fires.**

## Preventing forest fires

On page 30, you can find out how to help prevent fires breaking out at home. Take the following precautions in a forest:

1. Never light a fire or strike a match unless it is an emergency.

2. Never toss a burning match or cigarette on to the ground.

3. Never leave a fire or camping stove unattended.

4. Always make sure that a fire you have built is completely dead when you have finished with it by covering it with earth. Make sure you do not mistake leaf mold for earth: it looks very similar, but flares up when ignited.

## Extinguishing a fire

Remember: only attempt to put out a fire if it is small and you are sure you can control it. You could smother it, for example with a blanket or coat, or use a fire extinguisher. Also, if the fire does not involve electricity or oil, you could drown it in water. If in doubt about the reason for the fire, don't use water; you could do more harm than good.

**WARNING!!**

NEVER throw water on an electrical appliance, even when switched off. The electrical charge can kill.

1. Release any locks.
2. Aim towards the base of the fire.
3. Squeeze the handle.
4. Move the extinguisher to the left and right.

## Fire extinguishers

There are many sorts of fire extinguisher, suitable for different kinds of fire; always check yours before using it. Some contain water, so are not suitable for electrical or oil fires; others are designed especially for them. The most useful ones are multi-purpose extinguishers, which can be used to put out most kinds of fire.

# Making a fire

Although fire is potentially very dangerous, it could be essential in a survival situation. It can provide warmth and light, dry your clothes, enable you to cook food and purify water, keep animals and insects away, and signal for help (see page 38). Below you can find out how to make and control a fire. In many areas it is illegal to light a fire. For this and safety reasons, only light a fire in an emergency and make sure you know how to extinguish it (see page 27) before you light it.

## Location

Choose a sheltered place out of the wind in which to build your fire. If you are on open ground, you can create a sheltered spot by digging a trench and lighting your fire in this (see right).

If you are sheltering in a cave, build a fire at the back of it. Smoke from the fire will then rise up to the roof, leaving the air you breathe less smoky.

Never build a fire near the mouth of the cave, as smoke will probably be blown back inside. You may also be trapped inside the cave if the fire gets out of control.

**Fire at the back of the cave.**

## Choosing your materials

To make a fire which catches quickly and keeps going for as long as possible, you need to collect tinder, kindling and fuel.

### Tinder

Tinder catches fire easily, so is used to start the fire off. Examples include birch bark, dried grasses, pine needles and bird down. They must be bone dry to work effectively.

### Kindling

Kindling should flare up quickly, producing large flames which are used to set light to fuel. Examples include small twigs and soft wood (such as pine, spruce and willow).

### Fuel

Fuel is the main bulk of the fire. It gives off a lot of heat but burns slowly, keeping the fire going for some time. Examples include hard wood (such as oak, beech and hickory), animal droppings and coal.

## Safety first

Before building and lighting your fire, check the following:

1. If the fire were to get out of control, would you know what to do? (See page 27.)

2. Is the location far enough away from trees, bushes and other vegetation that might catch fire?

3. Is all your equipment and clothing well out of the way?

4. Do you need to do anything which would force you to leave the fire unattended? If so, do it first.

5. Have you water or a blanket handy to use in case the fire gets out of control (see page 27)?

## How to build a fire

1. Clear a large space around the site so that the fire will not spread. Collect a good supply of tinder, kindling and fuel.

**Clear space**

**Leave gaps to allow air to get through.**

2. Stack your tinder with the smallest pieces at the bottom. Surround this with kindling, placed vertically in a cone shape just above the tinder.

3. When the kindling has caught, gradually add the fuel, starting with the smallest pieces. Do not pile on too much at once: you may smother the fire.

To make a fire last overnight, place large logs over it. After about half an hour, cover it lightly with ashes and then dry earth. Make sure you do use earth, not leaf mold (see page 27).

**Your fire should still be smoldering in the morning.**

## Fire-lighting devices

### Matches*

Do not allow the match to blow out before you have lit the tinder. Crouch down and strike the match near the tinder.

### Knife and flint

To make a spark, hold the knife** and flint just above the tinder. Scrape the knife on the flint in a downwards motion. The sparks should set light to the dry tinder.

### Sunlight and lens

You can direct rays of the sun through a lens (such as a camera lens or magnifying glass). If the sun is strong enough, it will ignite the fire.

*See page 46 for advice on making your matches waterproof.
**Do not risk ruining your only knife by lighting a fire in this way.

29

# Survival in the home

Thousands of accidents involving electricity, gas and water occur in the home every year. You can help to avoid accidents in your own home by taking the precautions outlined on these two pages and by acting quickly and effectively in an emergency.

On the opposite page there is some useful advice on how to prevent a burglar or intruder from entering your home.

## Electrical safety

Carelessness with electrical appliances can result in severe electric shocks and fire.

★ Do not overload power sockets – ideally, you should only use one plug from each socket.

★ Do not use the cord to pull a plug out of its socket.

★ Do not twist or bend cords sharply.

★ Replace any electrical cords that are worn or damaged as soon as possible. Do not run cords under carpets or rugs; you will not notice if they become damaged.

★ Beware of second-hand electrical appliances – always have them checked by an expert before use.

Below there are tips on how to avoid accidents in your home.

★ Do not leave electrical equipment switched on and unattended.

★ Switch off and unplug your television at night.

★ Turn off your electric blanket before getting into bed.

★ Never use electrical appliances in the bathroom. If you have an electric razor, make sure you use a special socket.

★ Never dry clothes over an electric heater.

## Be prepared

Do you know how to turn off the electricity, gas and water supplies?

Do you know how to call the emergency services (police, fire or ambulance)?

Do you have the telephone number of your local doctor? Is it displayed by your telephone so that others can see it?

If the answer to any of the questions above is "no", act now. You will not have time in an emergency.

### Electric shock*

On the right, you can see what to do if you find someone who has had an electric shock.

### Emergency procedure

✳ Before touching the victim, check to see if he or she is still touching the appliance which caused the shock. The victim could transmit the electric current to you.

✳ If the victim is touching the appliance, stand on a surface which does not conduct electricity, such as a folded newspaper, and use a broom handle to separate them.

✳ Turn off the electricity at the plug or mains.

✳ Get help immediately and call a doctor.

*On page 27, there is advice on what to do if a fire breaks out through an electrical cause.

## Gas leaks

A gas leak is extremely dangerous for two main reasons. First, the fumes are poisonous and can kill you. Second, it could result in an explosion if the gas comes into contact with a flame or spark.

The first sign of a gas leak is the smell. If you smell gas, first check that it is not just a pilot light or burner that has gone out.

Emergency procedure
* Put out any matches or cigarettes.
* Do not touch electric switches.
* Turn off the main gas, electricity and water faucets, and extinguish the pilot lights.
* Tell everyone to leave the house.
* Open doors and windows.
* Call the emergency gas services from a neighbor's

Emergency procedure
* You can thaw a frozen pipe by directing hot air from an electric hairdryer at it. Hold the hairdryer at least 1ft away and put it on its lowest setting.
* If your pipes flood, switch off the main stop valve to stop any more water flowing into the pipes. Turn off the water heaters too, as the hot water tank may have drained.

## Frozen pipes

In cold weather, water inside pipes may freeze. This causes the water to expand and possibly burst the pipes. When the water thaws, your home may be flooded.

You can help to prevent pipes from freezing by wrapping an insulating material (such as felt) around them, and then wrapping plastic round on top of that. This is called lagging pipes.

## Crime prevention

Many unsuspecting people let criminals enter their homes, and are then robbed or attacked. Make sure that there is a chain or peep-hole fitted to your door so that you can see visitors before opening it fully.

Below there is advice on what to do if someone knocks on the door when you are alone in the house.

★ Do not let a stranger enter unless he or she has made an appointment and you are expecting the visit.

★ If you are expecting the stranger, ask for identification. If the person does not have any, or you are worried, telephone the head office and ask to speak to his or her controller. Alternatively, ask the person to come back later (suggest a time when there will be more people in the house).

★ Do not ever admit to being alone in the house. You could, for example, say that a friend or relative is in the bathroom or in the yard.

# Survival in the city

On most of the previous pages of this book, the natural elements are the major threats to your health and survival. However, in towns and cities you are more likely to be endangered by other people, in the form of harassment, robbery and assault.

On these two pages you can find out how to lessen the risk of being a victim, and what action to take if you are threatened.

## Trouble spots

The following places are particularly dangerous at night. If possible avoid them, especially when on your own.

1. Uninhabited side-roads. Stay on busy, well-lit streets if possible.

2. Areas known to be violent or rough.

3. Unlit areas.

4. Cul-de-sacs.

5. Underpasses.

6. Empty subway platforms. Stay close to the exit if you find yourself on a deserted platform.

7. Empty cars on the subway or train. Always sit close to the communication cord.

## Safety precautions

By taking the following precautions, you will reduce the chances of being threatened or attacked.

★ Never accept lifts from strangers.

★ Do not stay out very late, and do not walk home on your own. If necessary, call a taxi.

★ Do not leave home without knowing when the last trains and buses are running.

★ Take enough money for a taxi home, just in case you are stranded.

★ Facing oncoming traffic, walk along the center of the path. If you walk on the inside of the path, you could be pushed into alleyways and attacked.

★ Don't antagonize strangers.

★ Carry a shrill alarm (see opposite).

★ If you have a handbag, make sure it is securely fastened (see opposite).

## What to do if threatened

If you suspect that you are being followed, cross the road and carry on walking. Now check to see whether the person is still behind you. If he is, head for a place where there are other people and ask for help. However, only go for help at a house if there is a light on, or other signs of occupation. You could become trapped between the house and the attacker.

If someone actually threatens you, shout as loud as you can. Activate your shrill alarm if you have one (see right). Even if no one comes to help you, the attacker may become frightened or embarrassed, and go away.

You should always try to get away rather than risk confrontation. If in a group, try to keep together when running away. Keep your hands out of your pockets. They will then be free in case you have to defend yourself.

## What to do if attacked

On pages 36-37 there are a number of self-defense techniques which will help you free yourself and gain time to escape. In addition to these, use anything at hand to defend yourself; umbrellas and keys can both be very effective. If you are chased, put an obstacle between yourself and the attacker: a parked car is ideal. Stay on the opposite side until help arrives.

Pull the communication cord, if you are attacked on a train or subway.

## Helping the police

Below is a list of things to try to remember when reporting an incident to the police.

1. The approximate age, height and build of the attacker.
2. What clothes was the attacker wearing?
3. Did he have a beard or moustache?
4. Have you seen the attacker before?
5. What was the color of the attacker's eyes, hair and skin?
6. Did the attacker have an accent?
7. Any distinguishing features?
8. If a car was involved, what was its color, make and license plate number?

## Helping others

If you see someone who has been, or is being, attacked, think before you stop to offer help. You may be attacked yourself. It may well be more practical to alert other people, or to telephone for an ambulance or the police.

## Helping yourself

Below you can find out about shrill alarms. There is also advice on choosing and carrying a handbag to lessen the chance of having your pocket picked.

### Shrill alarms

These give off a high-pitched screech at the press of a button — loud enough to alert others and frighten an attacker away. Make sure that it is easily accessible, for example in your hand.

### Handbags

Choose a bag with a flap and secure fastener, and hold it tightly under your arm with the flap towards your body. Never carry your address and keys in the same bag; your house could be the next target of the thief. If threatened, give up your handbag rather than risk injury.

# First aid

First aid is on-the-spot treatment given to someone who is injured, while you are waiting for a doctor to arrive.* It is vital, since it can prevent the injury from getting worse and may save the casualty's life. Below is advice about first aid procedures for some common injuries. However, never try to treat injuries if you are not sure what to do – you could do more harm than good.

## I. Wounds and bleeding

Wounds break the skin, letting blood escape. Bleeding is caused by a break in one of the vessels which carry blood round the body. A break in a major artery or vein means a lot of blood is lost. This can result in shock and even death, so try to stop the bleeding as soon as possible.

**Treatment**

★ Raise the injured part and press on the wound to reduce the blood flow to the area. You may need to keep applying this pressure for up to 15 minutes.
★ Cover the wound with a sterile dressing (see above). If you do not have a dressing, use a piece of clean, smooth material, for example a handkerchief or a paper tissue.

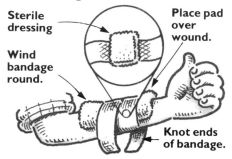

Sterile dressing

Place pad over wound.

Wind bandage round.

Knot ends of bandage.

★ Don't remove the dressing if blood begins to seep through. Bandage another dressing on top of the first.
★ Do not try to remove anything that is stuck in the wound (such as a piece of glass). You may do more damage by pulling it out.
★ If the casualty has lost a lot of blood, watch for symptoms of shock (see below).

## 2. Burns

Burns can be caused by naked flames, very hot or cold surfaces, chemicals, an electric shock or over-exposure to strong sunlight. A burn may look swollen and red, with blisters on the skin which, when they break, reveal a red patch which leaks fluid.

**Treatment**

★ Cool the burned area by holding it under cold, running water, or by soaking it in cold water for about 10-20 minutes.
★ Cover the burn with a sterile dressing (see above), or a clean handkerchief.
★ Watch for symptoms of shock (see right).
★ Get the casualty to a doctor.
★ Never apply any fats or ointments to a burn.
★ Never use adhesive plaster on a burn.
★ Never burst blisters caused by a burn.

## 3. Shock

Shock occurs when the body's organs are deprived of oxygen. This may be caused by a weakened heartbeat, which stops the blood circulating properly, or by severe loss of blood from either internal or external bleeding. Symptoms to look for are: turning pale; cold, sweaty skin; a weak, rapid pulse; shallow, fast breathing; yawning and sighing (through lack of air); loss of consciousness.

**Treatment**

★ Stop any bleeding (see above).
★ Lay the casualty down, with his or her legs raised slightly to aid circulation.
★ Loosen the casualty's collar and any tight clothes.
★ Keep the casualty warm but not too hot.
★ Get a doctor.

*As well as applying first aid, get medical help as soon as possible.

## 4. Broken bones

A broken bone (called a fracture) can be spotted from the following symptoms: a fractured limb may be twisted or bent at a strange angle, and the casualty will be unable to move it; the casualty may have been able to feel or hear the bone breaking; the area around the fracture may be swollen or bruised.

### Treatment

★ Do not move the casualty unless it is absolutely necessary. Never move someone who has injured his or her spine.
★ Keep the injured area still and support it by putting one hand above the fracture and one below it.
★ If it will take some time for a doctor to arrive, strap the injured part to another, unhurt part of the body, as shown below. Avoid bending the injured part.
★ Raise and support an injured limb when you have secured it. You could use a pile of clothing or a pillow for support.
★ Watch for symptoms of shock (see opposite).
★ Get a doctor.

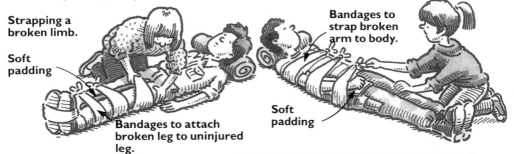

**Strapping a broken limb.**

**Soft padding**

**Bandages to attach broken leg to uninjured leg.**

**Bandages to strap broken arm to body.**

**Soft padding**

## 5. Heatstroke

This is caused by severe overheating, which causes the body's natural cooling system to break down. It happens most often in tropical climates, where conditions are often very humid and hot. Symptoms to look for are: dizziness; hot, flushed skin; a quick, strong pulse; high temperature; unconciousness.

### Treatment

★ Get the casualty to lie down in a cool place, and remove his or her clothes.
★ Sponge the casualty's body with cool water.
★ Fan the casualty.
★ Get medical assistance as soon as possible.

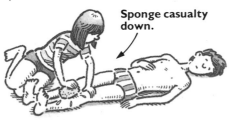

**Sponge casualty down.**

## First aid kit

A first aid kit is a vital part of your survival equipment. Even if you suffer no major injuries, your first aid kit will still be useful for treating any minor injuries such as small cuts, blisters or insect bites. Try to include the items listed below.

Sterile dressings.
Large triangular bandage (for slings).
Roll of bandage.
Adhesive plasters.
Aspirin.
Sunburn prevention cream.
Antiseptic solution and cleansing wipes.
Calamine lotion (for insect bites).
Germicidal soap (to sterilize your hands before treating injury).
Insect repellent.
Scissors.
Tweezers.
Safety pins.
Illustrated first aid manual.

# Self-defense

Below are a number of self-defense moves which can help you to break free from an attacker, and gain time to make an escape.* If one move does not work, you should quickly follow it up with another.

Do not practice these techniques unless you are under supervision from a qualified instructor. You could seriously hurt the other person. Instead, try to memorize the moves.

## Attacks from the front

The following moves are useful if the attacker is in front of you.

**Use this if the attacker has his hands around your neck.**

### Throat jab

Bring all four fingers of one hand in together and tighten your muscles so that the hand and wrist are completely rigid. Now sharply jab your fingers into the attacker's throat, as shown in the picture on the left .

### Leg pull

If the attacker raises his foot to kick you, turn your body sideways and cradle his leg in your arm. Now quickly pull the leg upwards until the attacker is off-balanced and falls to the ground.

**Use if your arms are free.**

**Use if one of your arms is free.**

### Eye poke

Use the two fingers closest to your thumb to form a V shape, holding the other two fingers with your thumb. Quickly bring them forward, and jab your attacker in the eyes.

### Knee blow

Bring one of your knees up as sharply as possible, and aim it at the attacker's groin or stomach. The most vulnerable part of the male body is the groin, so aim here if you can.

**Use if your arms are held.**

**Use if your arms are held.**

### Foot kick

Bring your foot back across your body to gain power, then kick the attacker as hard as possible on, or just beneath, his knee. You should use the outside of your foot for maximum impact.

### Thumb wrench

Pull your wrist away from the attacker and towards your body as forcefully as possible. Then drive your wrist sideways against the attacker's thumb, so that he is forced to release his grip.

**Use this if the attacker is grasping one of your wrists.**

*See pages 32-33 for advice on minimizing the chances of being attacked.*

# Attacks from behind

The following three moves can be used if your attacker is behind you.

### Finger twist

**Use this if the attacker has his hands around your neck.**

Pull back the attacker's little fingers as far as you can, twisting them as you do so. This is very painful, and should cause the attacker to release his grip on your neck. Quickly follow this up with another move, such as an elbow jab.

### Shin scrape and heel screw

Bending your knee, lift your foot up and firmly scrape your heel down the attacker's shin. Finish the move off by screwing your heel into his foot, or by stamping your foot on it.

**Use this if your arms are held.**

### Elbow jab

**Use this if one of your arms is free.**

Bend your arm and bring it forward; the farther forward you bring it, the more power you will gain. Twist to the side, clench your fist and jab the attacker in the stomach with your elbow.

# Some further techniques

Below are a few more techniques, including a simple but effective move for freeing your arms.

### Arm release

**Use this** ▶ **if the attacker is gripping your arms.**

Bend your arms, and bring your forearms up through the attacker's arms. Then push them outwards in a quick, sudden movement, thereby forcing the attacker to release his grip.

### Ground trip

**Use this if** ▶ **you are lying on the ground.**

If the attacker is kicking you, protect your head by cradling it in your arms. Twist to the side and block his kicks with one of your feet, then use your other foot to trip him up.

### Wall smash

**Use this if** ▶ **the attacker is grasping one of your wrists.**

If you are attacked in a city, it is likely that you will be close to a building. Use this to your advantage by pulling the attacker's hand back sharply against the wall.

# Signaling

If you are lost or stranded, it is important to attract attention as quickly and unmistakably as possible. There are many ways to signal for help: for example, a scrap of white or brightly colored cloth. waved in the air, or smoke from a small fire*, can attract attention. Below are some other signaling methods. Look for open, high ground to signal from: you will be more visible.

## Writing on the ground

A message written in large letters on a patch of open ground can be spotted by aircraft passing overhead. It is a good method to use if you cannot see any immediate sign of life in the surrounding countryside. You can then save your energy until you see or hear something that suggests there may be someone in the area who could help you. Then you can make more signals to attract their attention.

Look for a clear, level patch of ground on which to write your message. Remove anything that may

Need a doctor.

Need medical equipment.

Need water and food.

confuse it, such as loose rocks or fallen branches. In snow or sand you can simply scrape the outlines of your message on the ground. Otherwise, use materials that are lying around, such as sticks or

stones, to make letters (see above).

The letters SOS, and the ground-to-air signs shown above on the right, are recognized as distress signals throughout the world.

## Using a mirror

On a clear day, a flash from sunlight reflected off a mirror can be seen from up to 25 miles away. It is a quick, easy signal to make and is useful if you need to signal across long distances, for example from high up a mountain.
1. Hold the mirror at eye level, pointing at the sun so it catches the light. Decide on the target you want to signal at.
2. Hold your free hand out in front of you to arm's length, so that it is

between your mirror and the target, with the palm facing you. Part your fingers slightly so that you can glimpse your target through them.
3. Tilt the mirror until a spot of reflected light hits the place on your outstretched hand through which you can see the target.
4. Lower your hand, keeping the mirror still. The light should now be flashing directly at the target.

*See pages 28-29 for how to make a fire.

## Flares*

Hand-held flares burn as a bright light or trail of colored smoke which can be seen for miles. For this reason they are an excellent signal to use if you are stranded out on water, a long way from land, or if you want to attract an aircraft which is far away. Flares are effective both during the day and at night. When handling them, be very careful not to burn yourself. Follow these tips.

When using flares:
★ Keep them dry and away from any open flame.
★ Take only one flare out of its box at a time and put the lid back on when you have taken the flare out.
★ Read all instructions very carefully and make sure you understand them.
★ Make sure you are pointing the flare up towards the sky, away from anyone standing nearby.

★ Keep your face well clear of the flare.
★ Hold the flare at arm's length in one hand as you let it off.

## Body signals

If you have no signaling materials and can see potential rescuers who have not already spottted you, you can use your body to make signs which may attract their attention. This is a simple distress signal:

1. Stand upright. Raise both arms out to the side.
2. Lower your arms slowly.
3. Pause, then repeat the sequence.

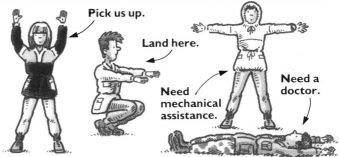

Pick us up.

Land here.

Need mechanical assistance.

Need a doctor.

Above are some more signals to make if you have managed to attract an aircraft and it is approaching. Make sure you copy these positions exactly, so that your message is clear.

## Morse code

Morse code is an international signaling language based on "dots" (short signals) and "dashes" (long signals). Various groupings of dots and dashes represent different letters of the alphabet, and so can be used to spell out messages. You can use many signaling methods to transmit a morse message, for example, you can combine short and long flashes from a mirror to make words, or blow short and long notes on a whistle. The morse alphabet is shown on the right.
  The morse SOS signal is ·········

A ·—
B —···
C —·—·
D —··
E ·
F ··—·
G ——·
H ····
I ··
J ·———
K —·—
L ·—··
M ——

N —·
O ———
P ·——·
Q ——·—
R ·—·
S ···
T —
U ··—
V ···—
W ·——
X —··—
Y —·——
Z ——··

*You can only use each flare once, so try to use one only when you are sure it will be seen.

39

# Using maps and compasses

One of the first things to do if you are lost or stranded in unfamiliar country is to take a good look around you for signs of civilization, such as buildings, which you could head for. If there are none, you could use a map to find out where you are and where to go. There is

some advice about using a map below.

If you have no map, you can recover your sense of direction by using a compass, or, if you don't have one, by using the sun or the stars. The opposite page and page 42 show you how to do this.

## Using a map

If you have a map of the area, you can find out exactly where you are and what sort of terrain, for example, hilly or marshy ground, lies round about. If you are going

on an expedition you need to learn how to read a map in detail. However, for survival purposes, follow these basic guidelines:

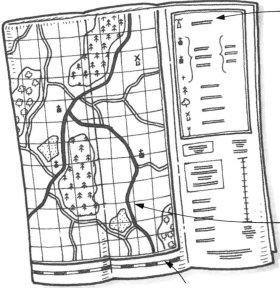

★ Most maps have a key or legend, which shows the various symbols used to represent features such as buildings on the map. To find where you are on the map:

1. Look at the countryside around you to see if you can spot any landmarks, such as roads, rivers, or forests.

2. Using the key, see if you can find these on the map.

3. Turn the map round until the places on the map line up with the real features you can see. You should be able to work out exactly where you are.

★ There should also be a scale marked on the map. You need to check this so that you can measure the distance between one point and the next. The scale is usually indicated either by a scale bar (showing miles or kilometers as they are measured on the map), or by figures expressed as a ratio, for example 1:760,320. If the scale is shown in this form, and the unit of measurement used is inches. this means $1/12$in on the map represents 63,360 inches (or one mile) in the actual landscape.

★ There may also be grid lines drawn vertically and horizontally on the map. A diagram on one edge of the map should tell you which direction is north. By looking along the grid lines that go in this direction you will know where north is (and so be able to place south, east and west too). You can then tell roughly in which direction any landmarks you can see around you lie.

If you can't see any landmarks, you can still use the grid to line up your map, or "orientate" it. Use a compass (see opposite), the sun or the stars (see page 42) to find north. Then align the grid line that runs north with this direction and you have orientated the map.

# Using a compass

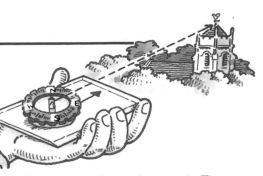

A compass consists of a magnetized needle which aligns itself with the earth's magnetic field and so always points towards north. A compass cannot tell you where you are, but it can show you which direction is which. This can be useful in several ways. For example, if you know that there is a road to the north, but you cannot see it, you can still reach it if you travel in the direction indicated by the compass needle.

To use a compass more precisely, you need to know how to take a bearing. This is the angle between a landmark and north, taken from where you are standing. To take a bearing:

1. Hold the compass level and flat. Keep it away from any metal objects, such as cameras. These may distort the magnetic field around the compass and so spoil the reading.

2. Allow time for the needle to settle. The colored end will swing towards north.

3. Adjust the dial of the compass so that the "N" mark on the dial lines up with the colored tip of the needle.

4. Look at a landmark. Imagine a straight line running from the center of the compass to the landmark.

5. On the compass, look at the point where your imaginary line crosses the dial. The number of degrees shown on the dial at this point is your bearing.

## Making a detour

If you have to make a detour as you travel, and lose sight of the landmark, use your compass to help you get back on course by following the method shown in this picture. The black line shows the route to follow.

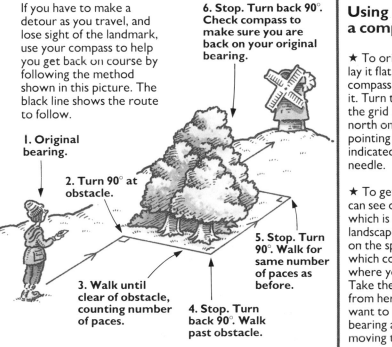

**1. Original bearing.**

**2. Turn 90° at obstacle.**

**3. Walk until clear of obstacle, counting number of paces.**

**4. Stop. Turn back 90°. Walk past obstacle.**

**5. Stop. Turn 90°. Walk for same number of paces as before.**

**6. Stop. Turn back 90°. Check compass to make sure you are back on your original bearing.**

## Using a map with a compass

★ To orientate your map, lay it flat and hold the compass steady just above it. Turn the map so that the grid lines that run north on the map are pointing in the direction indicated by the compass needle.

★ To get to a place you can see on the map but which is out of sight in the landscape, put the compass on the spot on the map which corresponds to where you are standing. Take the compass bearing from here to the place you want to reach. Follow this bearing and you will be moving towards that place.

# Using the sun

If you have no compass, you can use the sun to help you find your direction. You can do this because, as the earth moves round the sun each day, it follows roughly the same path. This means that at a particular time of day, the sun will lie in more or less the same direction as it did the day before. However, because the earth is moving round the sun, the direction in which the sun lies depends on which part of the world you are in. In the northern hemisphere (which includes Europe and North America), the sun is

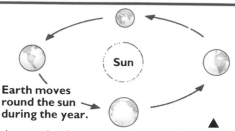

**Earth moves round the sun during the year.**

due south when it is twelve noon. In the southern hemisphere (including Australia and southern Africa), it is due north at this time. Use the method below to find out where north is at any other time of day.

★ Push a long straight stick upright into the ground.
★ Look to see where the tip of its shadow falls on the ground and mark this spot with a stone or twig.
★ Then wait at least fifteen minutes. The shadow will move round during this time. Mark the spot on the ground where the tip of the fresh shadow falls.

★ Draw a line on the ground between the two points. This is the east-west line. In the northern hemisphere, the first mark you made is west; the second, east. In the southern hemisphere, the first mark is east; the second, west.
★ To find north and south, draw another line at right angles to the first one.

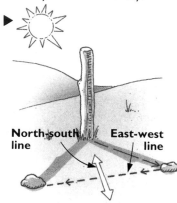

**North-south line**      **East-west line**

# Using the stars

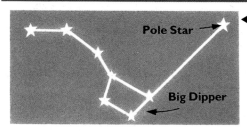

**Pole Star**

**Big Dipper**

◀ In the northern hemisphere, try to identify the Big Dipper (see left).* Imagine a straight line between the two stars on the far end of the "bowl" of the Big Dipper. This line points almost directly to the Pole or North Star, which shines roughly above the North Pole and is one of the brightest stars in the sky.

In the southern hemisphere, to find south, ▶ use a group of stars called the Southern Cross. You can find this group by looking along the mass of small, pale stars called the Milky Way until you come to a dark starless space. This is known as the Southern Coalsack. Just next to this space is the Southern Cross.

To find south, imagine the lines that form the Cross. Now find the star that marks the foot of the Cross. Imagine that the line of the Cross extends beyond this

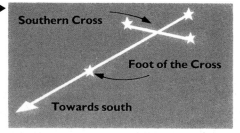

**Southern Cross**

**Foot of the Cross**

**Towards south**

star. You will then be looking towards the South Pole.

# Saving someone else*

In most survival situations, if your own safety is threatened, it is unlikely that you will immediately be able to do much to help anyone who is with you: you will be too busy saving yourself.

However, if you are safe but see someone in trouble in the water, or whose clothes are on fire, there are ways in which you can act immediately to save them without putting yourself at risk. These are situations in which any delay could prove fatal, so learning the rescue methods below could be crucial in helping to save someone's life.

## Saving someone from the water

When trying to save someone from the water, it is best to avoid entering the water yourself: you need to be a very strong swimmer to help someone if you are both in the water. Also try to avoid touching the victim: he or she may panic and grab you in an attempt to keep afloat. You can easily be pulled under by the person you are trying to save. Below are several methods of trying to save someone who is in the water while keeping yourself safe:

(1) Reach method. Stay on dry land, ▶ preferably lying down on your front, facing the victim. Try to "anchor" yourself firmly, either by holding onto something rooted like a tree, or by being held by another person. Then reach out towards the victim, preferably using something rigid and long such as a pole.

(2) Throw method. Stay on land. Throw either a buoyancy aid, such as a rubber ring, or something to catch hold of, such as a rope, to the victim. If using a rope, make sure you keep hold of one end.

(3) Row method. In a boat, don't try to haul a victim on board: you may capsize, or fall in yourself. Get the victim to hold onto the boat or to something held over the side. Row to shore.

## Saving someone whose clothes are on fire

Anyone who runs when his or her clothes are on fire fans the flames, making them burn more fiercely and quickly. Staying on your feet also means the flames can flare up into your exposed face. If you are at the scene of a fire and see someone running with burning clothes, or if your own clothes catch fire, follow the procedure shown here.

◀ Knock the person to the ground, using a shoulder charge. Avoid pushing them with your hands, which are less forceful and may get burnt. Try to keep clear of the flames.

◀ Roll the victim over on the ground. Try to cover him or her with a rug or blanket to smother the flames. Keep rolling until all the flames are extinguished.

*Try not to endanger yourself when rescuing someone. In many cases, the best thing to do is to alert other people, for example by telephoning the fire department or ambulance service.

# Getting to safety

As well as signaling for help (see pages 38-39), there are a number of things you can do to improve your chances of being found by potential rescuers. You can find out about these below. There is also some advice on how you can help your rescuers to save you most efficiently once they have arrived on the scene.

## Finding help

One of the first things you need to decide is whether to stay where you are, hoping that you will be found, or whether to move on and try to get to safety yourself. Here are some of the main points to consider.

★ Is civilization close by? If you can see signs of life or have managed to locate your position on a map, and you know how to keep to a course (see pages 40-41), it may be best to try to get to safety yourself. But if you don't know where you are heading, don't travel. You could wander round in circles for hours, exhausting yourself and getting nowhere.

★ If you have already been lost or stranded for several days and you have seen no sign of potential rescuers, moving on may be your only way to find help. You may also have to move on to find a fresh source of water.

★ Are you in a fit state to travel? If you are injured or exhausted and can find some shelter, it is best to stay put.

▲

★ How visible is your present location? If you are in an area where you will be easy to spot, for example on a hilltop, and you have water and a place to shelter, it may be better to stay where you are. However, if you are in a tropical jungle, where you will be almost impossible to find because of the dense vegetation, it is best to try to move to a more open area. If you have been involved in a vehicle accident, stay with the wreckage: it is much easier to spot than you would be on your own in the wild.

## Attracting attention

Whether you decide to go or stay, you need to make sure that you can attract the notice of any potential rescuers. Follow these tips:

★ Prepare signaling materials and be ready to signal quickly at any time (see pages 38-39), even if you are trying to travel to safety. You cannot afford to miss an opportunity of being rescued.

★ If you decide to move on, leave a clear, visible message at the place from which you set out, giving as much information as possible. Try to include details such as

your direction, the date and time, and the place you are aiming for.

★ Mark your route every now and then as you go, for example by leaving stones in arrow shapes indicating your direction.

▼

## Helping your rescuers

Rescuers often have to take considerable risks to come and save you. You can help them do so safely by following these suggestions:

★ Once you have been spotted or traced, and help is on its way, make your location obvious. Mark the spot, or repeat your signal. It is usually best to stay exactly where you were when your signal was picked up.

**Helicopter needs clear landing space.**

★ However, if you are being rescued by helicopter, make sure you position yourself away from obstacles such as trees, or places such as steep hillsides, where helicopters cannot land.*

### What to do when rescuers approach

1. Warn them of any possible dangers that they may not be able to see, such as crevices or loose boulders.

2. Follow the instructions they give you, such as keeping still. Be patient.

3. Tell them if you are injured, and where.

4. Try to keep calm: don't grab your rescuers so that they cannot move to help you properly, or so that you endanger their safety as well as yours.

## Dropping from a height**

If you are trapped in a room that is on fire, you may not be able to wait for help. You may have to leave through a window, which can involve dropping from a height. Never jump straight out of a high window. Instead:

★ Tie sheets or curtains tightly together to make a rope. Push some heavy furniture to the window, and tie the rope to it using a square knot. Drop the free end of the rope out of the window and lower yourself to the ground.

★ If you cannot improvise a rope, throw some bedding out of the window. Sit on the sill with your legs hanging out. Check that the landing area is clear. Grip the edge of the sill, turn round so that you are facing the building, and ease yourself down to arms' length.
  To drop, first release one hand and push away from the wall with it. Release the other hand. As you fall, cover your head with your arms and drop your chin on your chest. Close your mouth. As you land, bend your knees and move one arm across your body at head height to force you into a roll to break your fall.

*Don't approach the helicopter until signaled to do so.
**Never do this unless you are trapped by a fire.

# Survival kits

Having the right sort of equipment can help to save your life in a dangerous situation. Below are some suggestions for items to pack into different types of survival kit. The items shown and discussed here are just the basics: you will need to adapt your kit to suit the specific conditions you will be dealing with, how long you expect to be away, and how much else you have to carry.

## Essential items for all kits

Include the items listed below in all survival kits, whatever the size or type.

★ Waterproof matches. Drip melted candle wax over match heads. Allow it to cool. When you need to use the match, peel off the wax with your fingernail.
★ Strip of dry striking paper (cut off side of matchbox).
★ Candle for light, flame, cooking and warmth.
★ Compass.
★ Small mirror for signaling.*
★ Magnifying glass for fire-lighting.**
★ Small flashlight.
★ Sharp penknife.
★ Loud whistle for alerting rescuers.
★ Hard candy for energy.
★ Water collecting materials: plastic sheeting (preferably black), straws, water purifying tablets and a clean sponge for soaking up dew.
★ Razor blades (keep in a sealed box) for cutting things.
★ Needle and thread.

## Pocket survival kit

This kit should fit into a tin which snaps tight shut and fits into your pocket. Masking tape stuck round the edges of the tin seals it and can also be used in many other ways, for example, to patch holes in waterproof sheeting. Include the essential items, plus:

★ Flexible wire saw.
★ Flint and striker.
★ Aspirin and adhesive bandages.
★ Wire for fastening and cutting.
★ Safety pins.
★ Cleansing wipes.
★ Waterproof paper and pencil for messages.
★ Copy of morse code, first aid leaflet and drawing of solar still.
★ Map.

*See page 38.
**See page 29.

## Food*

Always take some food with you when going on an expedition. Here are some tips about choosing and storing survival foods:

★ Choose foods that give a lot of energy: carbohydrates, proteins and especially fats supply the most energy. You also need sugar and salt.
★ Carry a variety of foods to give you a balanced diet.

★ All food containers should be clean, waterproof, and sealed. Make sure cans are not dented or pierced, or the contents may be spoiled.
★ Dried, canned and powdered foods keep for longer than fresh food.

Just choose a few of the items listed here, to make sure your kit is not too heavy.

Canned beans.
Cookies and cereal bars.
Peanut butter.
Sticks or tubs of butter.
Nuts.
Cubes of dehydrated meat.
Canned fish and meat.
Hard chocolate.
Canned and dried fruit.
Sugar or hard candy.
Honey.
Salt.
Tea bags.
Powdered milk and soups.

## Survival pack

This is a more extensive kit suitable if you are going on a long journey. It provides you with some sources of shelter, food and warmth. Make sure the pack for this equipment is waterproof, strong, and fastens properly. Include the items from the pocket survival kit (see opposite), plus:

★ Mini flares. Pack in a waterproof bag and away from matches or any other inflammables.
★ Insect repellent.
★ Mosquito netting.
★ Sunscreen lotion.
★ Pencil flashlight will give extra light.
★ Tablets of solid fuel for fire-lighting.
★ First aid kit (see page 35).
★ Bivouac bag.
★ Space blanket. This is a lightweight, windproof and waterproof blanket which gives some insulation for extreme heat and cold. It is coated with aluminium on one or both sides to reflect heat or sun.**
★ Rope.

## Car survival kit

You should keep a survival pack (including a first aid kit) in your car. For long journeys, pack the extra items below.

★ Radio.
★ Jumper cables to recharge the car battery.
★ Flares
★ Spare tire, fan belt, bulbs.
★ Small fire extinguisher.
★ Big flashlight.
★ Shovel.
★ Tow rope.
★ Large plastic bottle of water.
★ Gas can with spare gas.
★ Can of oil.
★ Paper towels.
★ Windshield scraper.
★ Sunglasses.
★ Spare clothes.
★ Rugs and sleeping bags.
★ Tarpaulin.
★ Road maps and useful telephone numbers.

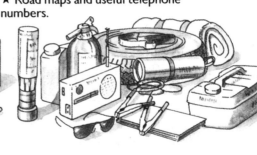

*Also take some drinking water stored in a clean plastic bottle.
**A space blanket can be used to make a shelter (see page 16).

47

# Index